Painting Songbird Carvings

16 Full-Color Plates and Complete Instructions

by Anthony Hillman

DOVER PUBLICATIONS, INC., *NEW YORK*

To the memory of
David Hillman

Published in Canada by General Publishing Company, Ltd., 30 Lesmill Road, Don Mills, Toronto, Ontario.
Published in the United Kingdom by Constable and Company, Ltd.

Painting Songbird Carvings: 16 Full-Color Plates and Complete Instructions is a new work, first published by Dover Publications, Inc., in 1988.

Manufactured in the United States of America
Dover Publications, Inc., 31 East 2nd Street, Mineola, N.Y. 11501

Library of Congress Cataloging-in-Publication Data

Hillman, Anthony.
  Painting songbird carvings.
  1. Wood-carving—Technique. 2. Birds in art. I. Title.
NK9704.H56 1988   731.4′62   87-27443
ISBN 0-486-25580-8 (pbk.)

Painting Songbird Carvings

AFTER YOU HAVE carved a songbird or purchased an unfinished carving, you will want to color it faithfully according to species. My purpose in creating this book has been to provide instructions and helpful tips to anyone who wants to paint a songbird carving, no matter what his or her preferred style of painting might be. I have included sixteen full-color plates of profile and top-view illustrations as a source of accurate information on songbird coloration. As of this writing, no publication has yet provided full-color top-view reference illustrations of songbirds. These plates show sixteen species of songbirds in their spring plumage, when colors are at their brightest. These colors may fade to varying degrees in the fall. The birds depicted here are males. In certain species, females resemble the males in most ways but have duller coloration. Examples of these are goldfinches and robins. In other birds, such as Red-winged Blackbirds and Purple Finches, females appear very different, showing no trace of the males' livelier colors. And in yet other cases, the plumage of both sexes is very much alike. Examples in this book include the Tufted Titmouse, Cedar Waxwing, House Wren, and Black-capped Chickadee.

Although these plates are the best painting guide available in book form and should be studied closely, the beginner cannot expect to be able to duplicate complex songbird coloration without some practice. Seldom can the exact color desired be squeezed right from a tube of paint. Many colors can be created only by the blending of pigments—and don't be afraid to experiment—but even basic colors vary depending on the type of paint (acrylics, oils, etc.) and the manufacturer.

Don't let this intimidate you. Study the instructions, plates and other sources carefully, and practice mixing and applying paints, but also do not be afraid to draw upon your own creativity. Discovering your own "recipes" is part of the fun of painting bird carvings. There is no one way to paint a carving. Gradually you will develop a personal style that you will be proud of.

RESEARCH YOUR SUBJECT

Before you begin painting, it is essential to study your subject carefully. Learn the different topographical features of a songbird (see Figure 1). This will help you remember where to apply the proper colors and markings. Feather shape and size often determine the color pattern, and therefore determine how you apply paint to your carving.

Study the color illustrations on Plates 1 through 16. These plates, which include both profiles and top views, may be removed from the book so that the appropriate one can be placed beside your carving and referred to as you paint. Supplement the plates with color photographs, any other illustrations you can find and, as much as possible, observation of live birds. This is not as difficult as it may sound. Many of the birds depicted in this book are frequent visitors to birdhouses, birdbaths and feeders. If you can observe a bird as it bathes, you will have an excellent opportunity to study at close range the groupings and structure of feathers that are common to all songbirds. In the summer, birdhouses will attract breeding birds of certain species, such as bluebirds and wrens. Feeders are especially good for attracting wintering birds such as cardinals, chickadees and titmice. If possible, place birdhouses and feeders near a convenient observation point—a window, for example (but out of reach of potential predators). Even if you are an apartment-house dweller in a large city, a trip to a nearby park in spring will, at the very least, afford you a close look at robins hunting for worms on the ground.

Thorough research is important, but I caution against just collecting photographs and other images without firsthand observation. Certain subtle aspects of form and color cannot be properly appreciated except in the living creatures themselves. Close study of these subtleties is therefore important, but it is also fun. Songbirds are a lively group of birds that are readily seen close at hand.

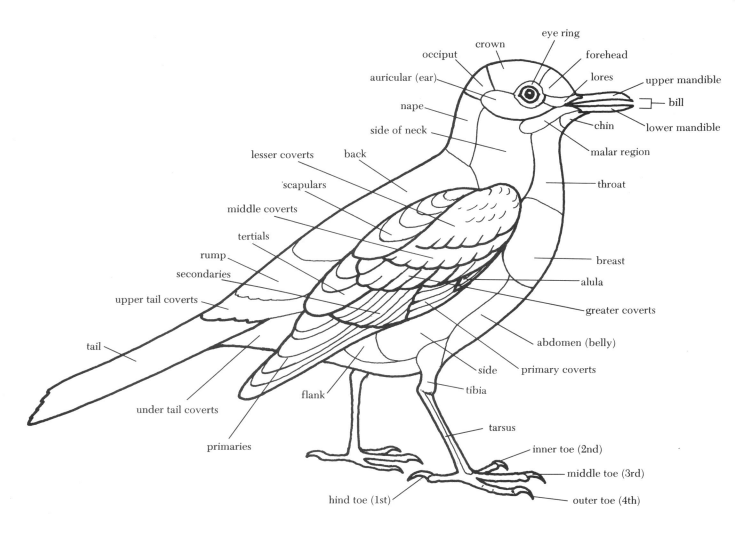

Fig. 1. Topography of a Songbird *(American Robin)*

With practice and observation, you will gradually find it becoming easier to paint realistically.

BRUSHES AND PAINTS

When choosing any art supplies, a good rule to follow is to buy the best, or at least the best you can afford. This rule applies especially to brushes, since the brush is the instrument that gets the paint onto the surface of your carving. A wide variety of brushes is available for any paint medium you use. Figure 2 illustrates some types of brushes I find useful for painting bird carvings. If brushes of the type you desire are not available locally, write for catalogs from some of the major art-supply firms. It will be futile to attempt to paint with inferior brushes.

Through the years I have become partial to sign-painting and lettering brushes. The longer bristles on these brushes hold more paint and make it easier to control long, delicate lines. They also help keep paint from getting up into the ferrule, an important advantage when working with acrylics (for which your brush also should have a soft, white, nylon type of bristle).

The "fan blender" is another useful brush, both for blending colors and for "dry-brush" technique. With this type of brush, I prefer white oil bristles, even for acrylic paints, as the stiffer bristles maintain the proper fan shape.

For applying large, solid areas of color, the larger-size "flats" (brushes with flattened ferrules) are the most useful. These brushes deliver a large quantity of paint while allowing good control where sharp edges are desirable.

In time you will find that some of your brushes are losing their shapes, their hairs twisting in every direction. Save these worn-out tools. Although they may no longer serve the specialized purposes you purchased them for, they can be invaluable for stippling and dry brushing.

Just as different kinds of brushes serve different purposes, different types of paint have different properties and produce different effects. Oil paints have the major disadvantage of taking a long time to dry. This can also be an advantage, however, as it permits colors to be blended to perfection. And if you make a mistake, the area can be

(Instructions continue after plates.)

Plate 1.   American Goldfinch

Plate 2.   Blue Jay

Plate 3. Red-winged Blackbird

Plate 4. American Robin

Plate 5. Northern ("Baltimore") Oriole

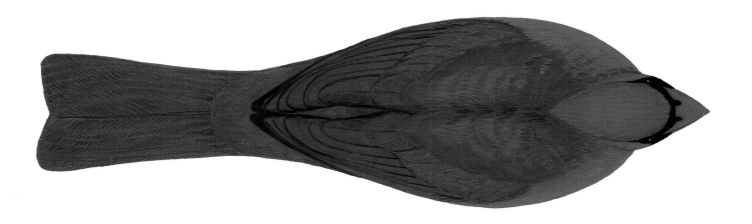

Plate 6.   Northern Cardinal

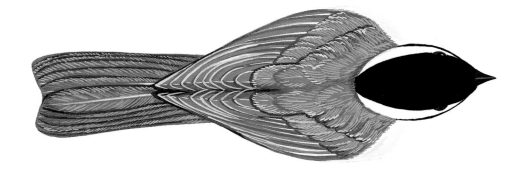

Plate 7.   Black-capped Chickadee

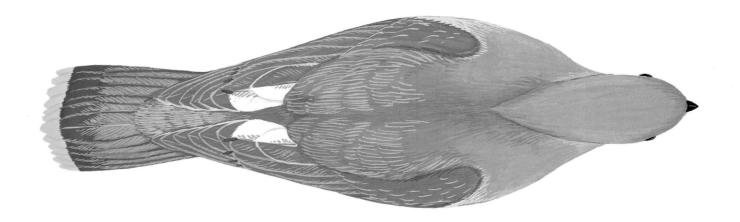

Plate 8.   Cedar Waxwing

Plate 9. Evening Grosbeak

Plate 10.　Eastern Bluebird

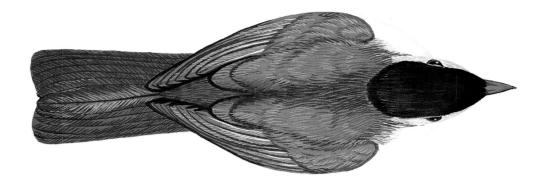

Plate 11. Tufted Titmouse

Plate 12. Prothonotary Warbler

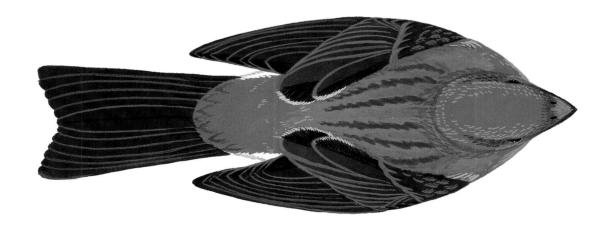

Plate 13.   Purple Finch

Plate 14.   Western Tanager

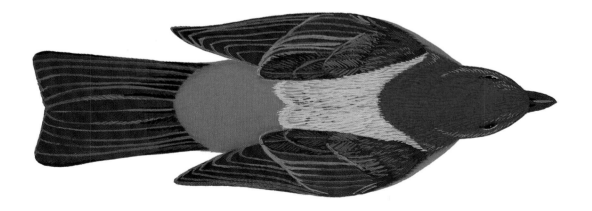

Plate 15.   Painted Bunting

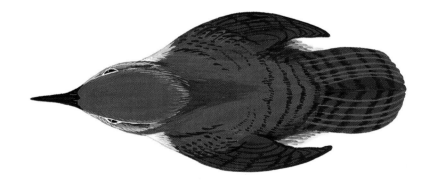

Plate 16.   House Wren

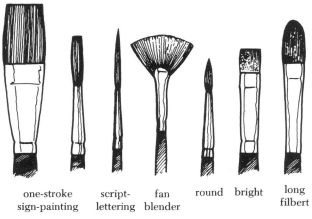

one-stroke   script-   fan   round   bright   long
sign-painting   lettering   blender   filbert

Fig. 2. Types of Brushes

wiped clean to start over again. If drying time is of no concern, you may prefer oils, for they produce a rich, almost sensual, gloss that seems to be obtainable with no other medium.

The two basic media for oil paint are turpentine and linseed oil. Turpentine will reduce drying time and deaden the sheen inherent in tube colors. Linseed oil, when added to paint, extends drying time and adds sheen. Several drying agents, such as cobalt drier, are available. Allowing oil paints to stand overnight on absorbent brown paper (like that used to make shopping bags) will drain off some of the linseed oil, as is preferred by some wood carvers.

Acrylic paint is probably the medium most widely used by carvers of birds. It dries quickly, and brushes can be cleaned in soap and water, making acrylics more convenient than oils for most people. *It is important to remember that for acrylic paints you must use acrylic primer.*

The speed at which acrylic paints dry can be a handicap for the beginner, but practice and familiarization with the medium soon overcome this difficulty. A gel medium, available in art-supply stores, slows drying time when added to tube acrylic paints.

Tube acrylics tend to dry with a slick surface. This is not necessarily desirable. I use flat exterior house paints as the main colors of my palette. Flat acrylics offer a distinct advantage when you are painting undercoats and thin washes of color, there being less chance of running or puddles of pigment remaining when the brush is lifted off the painting surface. Another advantage is that when additional markings are applied, as in feathering, the flat finish takes the applied color better.

Usually house paints are sold in quart cans. You may find it awkward to work from these directly, but transferring enough paint for several projects to smaller containers works fine. Basic colors available in flat house paints include black and white (from which you can also make gray) and brown. You may use tube colors and tints to achieve reds, blues, yellows, and other colors. This combination of house and tube paints is my personal preference. In any case, remember that it is easier to make the flat finish of a completed piece glossy (if you desire it) than to tone down a glossy finish to a soft luster.

SELECTING YOUR COLORS

If you have never painted a bird carving, start with a species that possesses a relatively simple pattern. Among the birds shown in this book that are suitable for a beginner are the American Goldfinch (Plate 1), Black-capped Chickadee (Plate 7), Eastern Bluebird (Plate 10), and Tufted Titmouse (Plate 11). As the American Goldfinch is one of the most widely distributed, best-known songbirds in North America, I will give detailed instructions for painting this bird. These instructions will also serve to suggest the general procedure for painting any bird carving. (For those who want to begin with the Black-capped Chickadee, another familiar songbird, detailed instructions may be found in my book *Carving Favorite Songbirds,* Dover 25358-9.) After the instructions for painting the goldfinch, I have provided a list of specific colors you will need for painting the fifteen other birds. Remember that this list is not fixed and absolute; many colors can be created by mixing others. The following colors, however, are fairly basic and are needed for all or at least most of the species illustrated:

1. White.
2. Black.
3. Burnt umber. (With flat house paints you must check color samples, as each manufacturer may market several brown shades under different trade names. An example is Cook & Dunn's "Cape Cod Brown," an excellent dark brown once a small amount of black has been added.)
4. Burnt sienna.
5. Raw sienna.
6. Indian red.

With the addition of a medium gray (which you may create, of course, by mixing black and white), these colors will provide the painter with the bulk of what he needs. Other colors necessary in smaller quantities include:

7. Ultramarine blue. (Check paint samples available; other types of blue, such as Prussian blue, cobalt blue or even Payne's gray—a bluish gray—may be more suitable to your immediate needs.)
8. Cadmium yellow, medium. (The various yellows should all be considered, depending on the species being painted. Yellow can be of primary importance in painting warblers and certain other species.)
9. Hooker's or deep green. (Many warblers and females of other species will require a mixture of yellow and green.)
10. Red. (Note: Most tube colors that look like "fire-engine red" are sold under such trade names as "Grumbacher red," "Winsor red," etc. Be sure to check color samples before purchasing.)
11. Cadmium orange, medium. (Whenever possible, I prefer to create the desired shade of orange by mixing cadmium yellow, medium, with red.)

Besides actual paints, a wide variety of colors is available in tints. The Rich Lux Products Company of Philadelphia puts out an excellent line known as "Minit Tint." The beauty of tints is that, since they contain no hardeners or driers, they have an extremely long shelf life under moderate temperature conditions. Be sure to follow instructions to determine the maximum amount of tint that can be safely used. Applying too much will prevent proper drying.

BEFORE YOU BEGIN

After you have sanded your carving to a smooth finish, it is necessary to seal the wood. Clear wood sealers include lacquer and shellac. Two coats are usually sufficient. Sand between coats with #220 or finer sandpaper. Wood that contains knots needs to be carefully sealed, as the resins in knots will discolor paint.

Once it has been sealed, your carving should be primed. Priming further protects the wood and provides a uniformly pigmented surface to paint on. Remember to use oil-based primer when you are painting with oils, acrylic primer when you are using acrylic paints. When you paint with acrylics, you may want to start with an oil primer and then coat this with acrylic primer. Acrylic primer applied directly to the wood raises the grain, an effect you may prefer. This requires more sanding, but it allows the natural beauty of the grain to show through.

"Kilz," made by Masterchem Industries, is an excellent product that I recommend. Since this is a primer-sealer, it allows you to prime and seal in one operation, saving you a step. Best of all, it can be covered with either oils or acrylics. When using acrylics, however, it is a good idea to top it with a coat of acrylic primer.

While brushing on any coat of primer, be sure not to leave ridges or brush marks, the presence of which will make painting of details more difficult later on. After the primer has dried, sand a final time with #220 or finer sandpaper. This will remove any roughness, providing a smooth base to paint over.

NOTE: Read and follow the instructions found on the labels of all primers, sealers and paints you may use. Familiarize yourself with the qualities of each product as well as precautions necessary for their safe use.

PAINTING A SONGBIRD CARVING— STEP BY STEP

Now you are ready to paint your songbird carving. The following detailed procedures for painting a male American Goldfinch in spring plumage, a brightly colored bird with only a few different areas of color, will give you a good idea of how to go about painting any songbird. It is advisable to read through all the instructions first, before actually mixing or applying any paint.

Referring to Plate 1, outline on your carving the boundaries of the major feather areas and the eyes, using an ordinary lead pencil. Do not indicate any finer details at this time. Always paint the areas that have lighter, brighter colors first, in this case the yellow body. If by accident you make the yellow too extensive, you can always paint over it in black, whereas if you need to paint over black with yellow, it is difficult to retain a strong yellow finish.

The basic color for the body of the goldfinch is cadmium yellow, medium. Depending on your preference, you may wish to lighten this color by adding a small amount of white. Give the body (except for the under tail coverts, which should remain white) two coats of this yellow. Let dry thoroughly between coats, checking for streaking after the first coat. If you feel confident that you can handle the fine detail, you may wish to paint the highlights and shadows as shown on the plate. For the lighter areas, use the basic body color, mixing in a little white. The color for the darker areas can be mixed by adding red (or a very small amount of burnt sienna) to a separate quantity of cadmium yellow, medium.

When you are satisfied with the appearance of the yellow areas of the body, paint the bill flesh color. Create this color by adding small quantities of red and burnt sienna to white. You will notice that I am not advising you to buy a tube of ready-mixed flesh-colored paint; colors of this nature that you mix yourself are usually superior to the ready-made product. The bill will probably also require a second coat of paint.

You are now ready to paint the wings, tail and forehead, using black. I caution you to be extremely careful when painting the edges of black areas. Having to overpaint in yellow an area mistakenly painted black is to be avoided at all costs. Let dry and check for streaking. You will probably need a second coat.

Now use a very fine-pointed brush to paint the eyes in brown, black and white. Fine markings on the wings and tail may be added in white and gray. For the legs, use the same flesh-colored paint that you used for the bill. Congratulations! If you have correctly followed all instructions and the color plate, you should now be looking at a fully painted carving of an American Goldfinch.

A word of caution to those who are painting carvings with wood-burned feather detail: make sure that the paint you use is of a consistency thin enough not to clog the fine details of feathering that you have so laboriously striven to create.

With practice you will acquire familiarity with the effects of different paints, tools and procedures. Do not strive for speed; it will come on its own. Depending on the degree of realism you desire, the color schemes shown on the plates can be either simplified or refined through further research and observation. Good luck!

For your convenience, the colors of the paints needed for the carvings illustrated on Plates 2 through 16 are given below. Remember, however, that pigments vary from manufacturer to manufacturer and with the type of paint. In many cases you will need to experiment with different mixtures to achieve a particular color. Some of the colors listed may be created by mixing others. And you may work out any number of satisfactory substitutions. The following list is intended only as a rough guide.

LIST OF COLORS

Plate 2. Blue Jay: Black; white; ultramarine blue; Thalo blue; burnt sienna.

Plate 3. Red-winged Blackbird: Black; cadmium yellow, medium; red; Prussian blue.

Plate 4. American Robin: Black; white; cadmium yellow, medium; burnt umber; Indian red.

Plate 5. Northern ("Baltimore") Oriole: Black; white; red; cadmium yellow, medium; cadmium orange.

Plate 6. Northern Cardinal: Black; white; red; red-orange; Davy's gray.

Plate 7. Black-capped Chickadee: Black; white; burnt sienna.

Plate 8. Cedar Waxwing: Black; white; red; raw sienna; cadmium yellow, medium; Payne's gray.

Plate 9. Evening Grosbeak: Black; white; burnt umber; cadmium yellow, medium.

Plate 10. Eastern Bluebird: Black; white; red; burnt sienna; Prussian blue.

Plate 11. Tufted Titmouse: Black; white; burnt sienna; blue.

Plate 12. Prothonotary Warbler: Black; white; blue; green; cadmium yellow, medium; red.

Plate 13. Purple Finch: Black; white; red; burnt sienna; burnt umber.

Plate 14. Western Tanager: Black; white; flame red (orange-red); cadmium yellow, medium; burnt sienna.

Plate 15. Painted Bunting: Black; white; Prussian blue; Ultra blue; cadmium yellow, medium; Thalo green; flame red; burnt sienna; burnt umber.

Plate 16. House Wren: Black; white; burnt sienna; burnt umber; yellow ochre.